PET

THE
FIVE PILLARS
OF
RELATIONSHIPS

(Five Pillars of Inner Wisdom and Love in Relationships)

Contact us for any products, services, or 'relationship building':
www.FivePillars.ca
www.HealYourself.ca
Telephone 250-382-9397

Note for Librarians: a cataloguing record for this book that includes Dewey Decimal Classification and US Library of Congress numbers is available from the Library and Archives of Canada. The complete cataloguing record can be obtained from their online database at:
www.collectionscanada.ca/amicus/index-e.html
ISBN 1-4120-5291-2
Printed in Victoria, BC, Canada

Printed on paper with minimum 30% recycled fibre. Trafford's print shop runs on "green energy" from solar, wind and other environmentally-friendly power sources.

TRAFFORD
PUBLISHING

Offices in Canada, USA, Ireland and UK
This book was published *on-demand* in cooperation with Trafford Publishing. On-demand publishing is a unique process and service of making a book available for retail sale to the public taking advantage of on-demand manufacturing and Internet marketing. On-demand publishing includes promotions, retail sales, manufacturing, order fulfilment, accounting and collecting royalties on behalf of the author.

Book sales for North America and international:
Trafford Publishing, 6E–2333 Government St.,
Victoria, BC v8T 4P4 CANADA
phone 250 383 6864 (toll-free 1 888 232 4444)
fax 250 383 6804; email to orders@trafford.com
Book sales in Europe:
Trafford Publishing (UK) Ltd., Enterprise House, Wistaston Road Business Centre,
Wistaston Road, Crewe, Cheshire cw2 7RP UNITED KINGDOM
phone 01270 251 396 (local rate 0845 230 9601)
facsimile 01270 254 983; orders.uk@trafford.com
Order online at:
trafford.com/05-0186

10 9 8 7 6 5

This book is dedicated to "Humanity"

"May we allow our children to continue to have
their visions and adults their dreams…"

FRIENDSHIP

**"May you start a new friendship today—a friend-
ship with yourself"**

With true friendship, we need to bring the best to each
other, and you must start first with Yourself.

Knowing where you are going in life requires visualizing
where you are and where you want to be—not investing
energy in the future and past, but allowing life to flow in the
present.

Other people's opinions are not important. What they
think is their opinion and where they see you—that is just
theirs. We all need to reduce our ability to judge others and
spend less time on controlling others.

We cannot be any good to anyone else until we first take
good care of ourselves.

Be your own best friend—and walk your talk. It is in
taking one step that we may take two. We are then able to go
on slowly without fear. Remember, the longer the wait, the
bigger the prize.

As Peter's grandmother once said, "pian piano si va londano"—slowly, slowly, you shall go far...

Trust yourself and know your true self will guide you wherever you go.

To be your own best friend and know you are one with all.

Our eyes are our windows to our soul—so laugh lots...it puts a twinkle to our eyes. Be thankful and laugh lots—it is the window to the soul, and it heals our Self.

May we never take anything for granted and be thankful
for all we are—all we have—and love rather than
fear life. And most of all, forgive thyself of these
three. Forgiveness will grant us peace and prosperity
in our lives and in our World.

THE FRIENDSHIP AND KINDNESS POEM

Kindness creates miracles
"Be kind to yourself in friendship"

Your kindness creates miracles

"Your calmness and clarity are easy to find—our love and friends, our care and understanding—Once we look within ourselves and find what we have been looking for all along—within ourselves—just waiting to be awakened, brought alive again—and listened to once again."

Your kindness will always create miracles

Always be kind to yourself in friendship

CONTENTS

Friendship v

The Friendship And Kindness Poem. vii

Forward xi

Preface xiii

Introduction 1

Caveat And A Note From The Author 9

I   Know Thyself. 13

II   Master Thyself. 27

III   Give Thyself — 35

IV   Love Thyself 61

V   Trust Thyself Trust Yourself 73

Afterword 81

Acknowledgements 83

About The Author: 105

FORWARD

In this book, "Five Pillars of Relationships," Peter Sammarco reminds us of those things in life that really matter, that have real value, and how to get in touch with them again. He reminds us how these issues are interrelated and universal. He reminds us that we all have an inherent pure nature and how we long for peace, love, health, honesty, justice, and care. He speaks of the need of duty and commitment to bring these values alive.

Peter speaks not from the mouth, but from the heart. As one of the chaplains of the Interfaith Chaplain's Services at the University of Victoria and as his spiritual advisor, I have watched Peter grow and develop spiritually. I have the deepest respect for him. Peter walks the spiritual path that is open to all of us, but few follow.

His multi-interests, and especially his compassion, which gives him a deep understanding of Interfaith and insight in the mystics of the Soul, combined with his personal efforts to succeed, make this book such a jewel, and a guideline for those seeking the simple, but deep spirituality in their lives.

It will help beings to understand each other better, love each other more, and become better beings in the process.

I highly recommend this book as one of the literary highlights of the year.

Lama Margaret Ludwig

PREFACE

Peter Sammarco shares his great ability to "Bring people together" and is able to see all points of view in Any Situation – He says "it's Never the issue that is the problem, But rather it is the attitude toward the issue at hand."

He loves to help others understand each other and when he ran for office, coined the phrase, "Bridging Cultural Diversity" and the Commonalities that we all have. Peter Believes that it is in our differences that we are Best able to See each others Commonalities – and this Book *Bridges Beautifully* the Differences that we think we all have between our minds and our hearts ~ until we realize that we are one. This he shares to all with Love.

INTRODUCTION

"It is in knowing who you are that you are better able to see yourself"

The purpose of this book is to help you to work on your relationship with Yourself. These pillars will discuss not so much the purpose of personal relationship with others, but rather the relationship you have with Yourself. God is in our hearts.

How can you help yourself to grow? Well, by being willing to find out who you are, by being willing to look at Yourself, and allowing this self-awareness to lead to new levels of consciousness and personal growth.

The next step is your commitment to change them, for simple awareness alone will only work once one's power of intention is to change, to improve, and to grow step by step, on a daily basis. This willingness to grow and learn, or most commonly re-learn and undo old ways, patterns, and belief systems, to change old behaviors, and acquire and maintain new skills in life, requires a shift in paradigm (to see things another way). The willingness to transcend one's past and

1

live in the "the present time" or "the present moment" is very important.

It is equally important to love now, forgive now, love and live and laugh today. By just smiling, our whole physiology changes in less than an hour. Smile for a month and see what happens—or say hello to strangers for no reason but to show kindness and self-love. This shows the self-love we have and demonstrates our ability to share that love with others. Pretty simple, don't you think? **Recognize people for who they are!**

Truly, we have taken steps to self-love, once we are willing to get to know ourselves. In doing so, we accept our shadows, embrace them, and let them go. In letting go, we develop our personal characters and identities. We also improve our self-image, knowing we are all images of the creator, capable of changing and doing anything in our lives once we believe in ourselves. We all must work toward the betterment of this process called Life, working with the God within us that knows all things and heals and grows all things with Love.

Healing our bodies is not an intellectual process. Our hearts heal our minds for the spirit of enthusiasm to heal comes from within us. The word "enthusiasm" means "zeal" as inspired by the spirit of God. With the Spirit of God within us, we can heal our own bodies. Explain that one to medical science!

Ruling our bodies means taming our minds and listening

to our spirits or our hearts. Our intuition is truly God within us talking to us directly. Anyone who masters their mind knows that their heart controls their destiny and journey. Mastering ourselves means listening to our hearts. Do you want to really listen to the voice of God within? Spend one full day and night just in silent prayer, or just listen—take time for yourself. Unplug all the phones. No T.V.—just listen. Maybe occasionally some music to guide you. But even that takes you away from Silence. So better still, keep in Silence and know God is in You.

> *Listening to your voice in Silence Now that is*
> *empowering yourself -*
> *Listening to your inner voice.*
> *It knows what to do.*
> *Your voice knows everything already*
> *Your voice knows what to do*
> *Listen to your voice in Silence.*

Wash dishes and just pray—for every dish you wash pray to one person. Feel it in your body. How does it make you feel to pray peace, wealth, affluence, and feel it in the body, as my good friend Nettie used to tell me. Try it—have fun with it. Life won't stop by taking one day off—24 hours just in prayerful silence. You will find the voice within you is God speaking to you directly. Try it—keep quiet for once and listen—do something that will really bring you peace, and from peace you will find a truly blissful spirit and your heart telling you how incredible you really are. Allow for mistakes, but truly we do not make mistakes—everything is divinely planned, especially 'loving thyself.' Pray success, wealth, and peace to all that you encounter.

Self-love is what you have displayed by opening the pages of this book. Thank you and God bless. Namaste (I honor the place where we both recognize we all are one).

Peter's sister, Isabella, knew how to live in the moment and to impact in a positive way as many lives she could touch with her strong love, kindness, firmness, and fairness. She knew she would die in her teens. In fact, one day, as a child, she asked our mother how long she would live before she died. This really impacted our lives—and it taught us how to live in the moment.

Isabella had compassion, caring for all others before herself. She rarely ever complained to anyone, except to a few friends and family. Most of the time her smile radiated across the room, and just her presence made gatherings and parties far more enjoyable, fun, and peaceful. There was a balance about her that calmed everyone around her. She had this ability even from a long distance. She was loved by all who sat in her presence. "Thank you, God, for God did more than loan us a wonderful angel—we lived with God for 14 years," as our father once said.

She had a fruitful, wonderful life, yet painful, until she

at last closed her eyes. After seeing our father come into the room, with one last tear running down her cheek, she took her last breath. She had been waiting for our father to come.

You must never think thoughts that take you away from your peace. Wisdom comes when our thoughts are always on the divine guidance within and know that all things work out in divine time and order.

Let your thoughts be ones surrounded by joy and love, for wisdom is knowing that any thoughts that take you away from your peace or bring you down in any way or lower your spirit must be avoided. Don't question yourself. Spirit is kept alive by knowing, not by questioning, your abilities. God helps all people succeed.

You must avoid any thoughts that truly bring your true spirit or level of energy down. This is true wisdom—not allowing any thoughts to bring you down in any way. This is why optimism or focusing on God's guidance or divine plan, or reading positive affirmations about yourself and others, are the first steps to enlightened wisdom of oneself to the people around you—pure and simple—yet simple and sweet. Our divinity lies within us all.

When we put limitations on our love, we destroy it. When we commit to grow through each other's faults, then the relationship flourishes. This does not come without excellent communication with one another. First, we must be able to be very honest with each other, especially ourselves—yet with honesty must come our ability to be unconditionally forgiving. Honesty breeds openness, yet this openness takes the lid off a "whole can of worms."

There is a tendency for us to look within and forget the potential and power we have within us. We are playing God, yet forgetting to act like God. Our human potential is to be God-like for we are all like God within. Once we tap into the incredible power, it is time to rule and to create our own life and Rule Thyself.

Spiritual sustenance based on spiritual principles is needed in every relationship in our lives. Many people feel they need personal counseling. That is fine—yet what they are really saying is that they need "spiritual sustenance" in their lives. Spiritual sustenance means our ability to live by spiritual principles, first and foremost in our relationships with ourselves and others.

One must realize that to master ourselves, we need to go beyond psychological and intellectual thought—logic alone will do nothing for a relationship. Thinking only with a calculated mind, figuring out what is good and what is less risky is where the trouble begins. Relationships are not black and white. There are plenty of gray/white zones. To combine love into your relationship one must find God in their hearts. Hearts rule relationships—not our minds. That is why the relationship with others must start first with ourselves.

It is our hearts that heal all things—never our minds.

Transcend the mind and listen to your heart. May we enjoy the journey together.

CAVEAT AND A NOTE FROM THE AUTHOR

Repetition is the key to learning.

Repeating to yourself something over and over again will reinforce it from your surface of your mind into your heart, where there is instant and constant permanent change.

Repetition is the ultimate key to any fundamental learning. If you want to remember something, it must be repeated at least several times a day. Why not repeat to yourself

Forgive thyself x ten times

or thinking only love or peace. This will transform you. **"Just thinking of someone you love will instantaneously heal you and your body because the feeling comes from your heart."**

"Visualize Peace" as our father does—Love Thyself—see yourself as a person who you Love—feel that feeling of love for yourself right Now—just today say "I Love you, (blank) and See how it will transform You.

Love is simple. So is Peace, understanding, and forgiveness if we use it Long enough and often enough. We have been so conditioned by negativity that we learn and find it so much easier to focus on negativity, that when we hear about love or peace, we become "pessimistic" (another negative thought)!

Catch yourself and see how just by asking for God's guidance you can stay with Peace almost all the time. When we love ourselves—peace comes naturally!

We are rich when we love ourselves.

Start with yourself. It is the key to success. Ultimately remember forgiveness is the key to success and affluence in our lives.

Put yourself in a state of Readiness—Breathe—take a deep Breath first. Allow yourself to Come to God—God is in you, So Close your eyes and feel the presence of God working through you and guiding you wherever you go—listen—standstill and listen to God in your heart. "God is with you wherever you go —"

You must take time to listen—you need not even listen—just feel. Know you are God, and **you can do anything.**

So here is the beginning of chapter one.

Listen, and know thyself completely.

> *We are unique and need to find and search for*
> *The purpose that is awaiting inside all of us.*
> *We need not even search—just listen —*
> *We need not even listen —*
> *Just find—we need not even find—just know.*

For we already have everything within us.
It's within each of us—the uniqueness to create
miracles.
Our feelings, thoughts, and words are our
prayers,
So select your thoughts carefully,
Believe in yourself and know yourself, for
In doing so, you know the Spirit that resides
inside each one of us.

I

KNOW THYSELF

"It is knowing who you are that we are able to see ourselves…"

Positive   Negative
Opinion   Opinion

Which one brings Peace?

"You may be right—but always choose the positive"

Choose always what will bring you closer to yourself, that will maintain your integrity and will bring you inner peace rather than discord.

Personal growth comes from seeing the "good" in all things and seeing the good in yourself. Be happy, smile, and **breathe**—believe and breathe deeply every day. But remember, breathing alone is not enough. Meditate and be aware of the conscious effort of your breath. **Meditation is one of several forms of prayer.**

Are you breathing in deeply every day or are you taking

low shallow breaths? Let your breath flow and **b-r-e-a-t-h-e.** It will propel you today and every moment of every day.

Read a book on yoga, the scientific study and power of breath. I read my first book on yoga in college when I was trying to satisfy God's presence dwelling in me and was searching for how I could improve my own vitality, health, and personal strength. Yoga and meditation and prayer work within us all. It teaches us how the eternal world has far more power over us than the external world. Master yourself through the power of breathing, meditating, yoga, and deep prayer. "For in silence so shall I be there, residing in you. For you and I are one." **Silence always brings us closer to ourselves. It is in breathing and connecting to our hearts that we create peace in our inner world.**

Realigning your thoughts to your heart, and feel your mind slowly being governed by that stillness and silence of your heart. Our minds produce tens of thousands of thoughts a day, many are repeated. We need to reflect on our thoughts and discover what we think of ourselves. This world has nothing more to offer than that which is within us. Our heart takes us away from our thoughts, and our thoughts take you away from your heart. Follow your heart—the desires of the heart heal you.

Breathe and pray—then meditate on any question you may have. For you will find God—once you find yourself within Silence. The Father will guide you and listen to your voice—as you pray deeply and concentrate on your breath. You will be guided to the answer that awaits in your time of Silence. "In silent prayer so shall I be there."

We are One

The blue sky
Way up high
Is one with us
Shine and fly.
Rap your thoughts
In beauty and see
In the end
It is all within.
We are One.

We care for one another and love one another as a family when we think of others, live in this moment, and give love from the heart. What we have is love—let's give from that love.

We build self-worth and self-esteem by building ourselves up, by praising who we are and what we can be. It's that simple! Yes, it all starts from within.

We are One

Feel the words spoken by others, in your body—even if you do not understand the words—just the presence of the person around will penetrate "vibrations of peace" in your body. Believe in yourself to listen and hear the words and feel them in your body. Your body is a very good indicator of the TRUTH. TRUTH comes from the Spirit that is generated through the vibrational form of our words—and just the presence of these words, no matter what language, will create the desired objective. *This powerful visual intent of our words is far more important than the words themselves—for the words hold an energy that we will feel in our hearts—which is in our body—which is stimulated by our Spirit.* **In the end the Spirit has the say, a vibrational form that creates all the answers to our circumstances.**

Farsi, Chinese, Italian, Japanese, French, English, Spanish, Swahili—what are these? They are modes of communication. How did these modes of communication come about? It is trembling vibrations, depending on the tone of our voices. We give or receive certain vibrations that we understand in a given language. Some tones are certainly cultural. How do you think we understand another person when that person speaks another language? Through the use of tones and the vibrations they transmit in their giving of sounds. It is not the language, it is the tone and energy used in the language that we understand one another. The energy is in our own voice and in our tone. It is vibrational energy that creates trembling in your body—it doesn't matter so much the words, but rather the vibration made by the words.

We understand ourselves by the vibrational frequency of our own voices, feelings, and the language we use for ourselves.

Realign and focus on what you want from yourself—what you are aware of will grow—so focus on what you feel in your body and allow new ways of thinking and feeling that will take its place instantaneously. You can even change the way you feel, by smiling or laughing (which increases endorphins), hugging someone, which increases your hemoglobin levels—giving you more energy and vitality. This makes you feel **HAPPIER.**

"Always keep your hands close to your heart"
You need to feel in your heart, not in your head
This helps us to grow to a closer humanity of
enlightenment and inner peace.

What you are is something that is within us all. These inner qualities of self-love, inner perspectives, and inner reflection are who we really are. As we look out at the world, what we see is what we get. If we think the world is a wonderful place, we will get more of this wonderful world around us and within us. No matter where we go, the more we love—the more we find we can love.

Love is love—there is no other meaning. Nothing could ever be close to that truth. Babies do not grow in knowledge and then say, "Okay, now I know who to love." We have the freedom to choose how we react to what happens to us in our lives. Someone may be directing their actions or behavior towards us that is kind or unkind, and we have the power and choice of how we respond to such behavior.

Let us always choose peace, which may mean not responding at all—just listening and letting go—like water off a duck's back. God is love and only love. Know thyself is a fundamental principle to knowing how to love and trust yourself. Once you know who you are, you have no possibility of hurting anyone else. Don't give me the excuse that business is business and that's the way it is. Business involves people—if you have no people, you have no business. You care for one another, not hurt your customers, partners, or clients. It is important to cooperate and not compete—send love and continued success to your competitors. Giving love to your clients is crucial to success, wealth, love, and a life worth living.

Continue to grow and to know who you really are. We do not mean your gender, your job, or your nationality. This means nothing to you and your inner Self.

Knowing yourself means being at the top of your corporate ladder wherever you may be. Knowing yourself leads you to master your self-worth.

1. Know you are complete. Here is an overview of knowing yourself.

    i) Ask yourself what kind of person are you Within

and truly listen to the answer. We All have the innate qualities as a child. It is important to go back and give time to nurturing yourself—refresh, restart, and regain confidence in yourself. It is in faith that you find your answers. Have faith in yourself and find your answers today.

ii) Listen to yourself. Listen to your inner voice. Close your eyes—ask positive, constructive questions and find the answers within.

iii) Do all this by just breathing.

iv) Give your subconscious mind something to play with every morning and every night.

I have built a goal sheet for dreams and desired projects that I wish to master or complete. It will happen by sharing with my heart what I need to know and what I need to do.

Repeat this a dozen times before bedtime and when you awaken in the morning, this will clear the pathways in your mind in order to achieve your desired objectives. It really works. Just create consistent and persistent visualizations of your goals, dreams, and desired objectives and projects. Simple stuff really.

v) Give yourself time to nurture yourself, to go out in nature, or just to take that bath and find yourself in silence. Your silence brings you back to God. What a better way, really, what a better way (yes, I said it twice) to go out and see it—for it will always seek you.

What you are attracting in your life depends on what you think about consistently on a daily basis. Water it with love and care, cultivate it with persistence and persevere in your visualization. Like the bamboo tree, it needs water every day before it creates roots to grow.

We need to grow with the times and embrace all forms of wisdom—for all lead to one TRUTH. The TRUTH is we are all one!

Who am I? What am I to do? Who am I really inside?

Am I a caring father, a loving mother, and an understanding person or teacher?

Do I smile a lot?

Do I pull jokes? If, when and why?

I AM NOT A WRITER. That's not who I am—this does not distinguish my identity. I am beyond any occupation or nationality. For who I am is beyond belief. For I know I am more than what I am, and again beyond what I even do.

God is in you and me. All around us.

I write.

I paint.

I exchange goods for money.

I love—and give love and receive love—just like breathing.

I paint wood and aluminum.

I share conversations with my parents, my friends, business colleagues.

I give love the most.

Most of all, love, yes, love all, to love all, we will give all love—and of only love to all, nothing else will matter. Nothing else will ever matter, just love.

We are talking about the ability to give love and accept and receive love from others.

We need to respect ourselves and others.

We need to not only accept others, but support our relationship with ourselves.

Can we love one another when we think of caring?

God is all around us and within us.

As we move on, we love ourselves enough to invest our thoughts and energy on what we value the most. By letting go of the past, we are allowed to live purely in this moment. (My sister knew how to live in the moment, and we learned from her how to love now, live now, forgive today. When energy was spent in being angry, we would always at some point apologize.)

> *Make the present moment yours with Love*
> *- friends hold each others dreams to the light*

By asking ourselves whether we are willing to break the chains of the past, we allow the new to take control completely. A new energy field then exists in all of us.

GOING Beyond Passion

We all need to believe in ourselves and have a passion for what we do every day. For many, life is believing in themselves—they live every single day as alive and willingly as possible. To live is to love with passion—to live with openness.

Again, by asking ourselves whether we are willing to break the chains of the past, we allow the new to take control completely. We must make this a powerful intention.

If I live my purpose and serve others, everything else will take care of itself in divine order.

God knows we are more than our personalities, gender, sexual orientation, religion, or nationality. These are all irrelevant. What matters is what's inside of us. Are we caring, loving, compassionate, and empathetic to others or are we just thinking what we can get for ourselves. Are you kind and keep your distance? What fills your mind with love—yourself, somebody, or something like television, a car, or a house?

Do you realize that love comes from your heart? Are you open or closed to loving others and yourself? Where do you put your energy or attention? Which matters most to you? How do you see your priorities in your life? Is your primary purpose to be rich or do you realize you are already rich with love, a sense of humor, intelligence, brilliance, and uniqueness that will astonish the world around you?

What I am saying is the world is in you—it is not out there—find a reason to pursue it. Find a service, not a job. Believe in yourself. Go within and find the guidance that will bring you closer to your purpose and service in life. It will fulfill you and keep you happy and at peace. Remember, when someone says something negative to you—doubt it—believe when you hear something good.

Most religions have no interest in helping anyone to get closer to God. How can we expect to experience God if one is constantly considered imperfect? We are perfect in God's eyes and in God all things are possible. Surely they want us to understand their teachings. How many religions tell you that you are God and God lives within you—that God is omnipresent in everyone and everything—to the smallest of insects that you see on the ground. There is only one truth and one power, and that is the power of God that is in us all. It is captured within us once we align with God's consciousness, through love, prayer, breathing, proper meditation. In silence we connect to God dwelling within us.

Love is abundantly clear—it gives. Love is in abundance. "It fills us up in God's image." Things on the other hand fill us up, but do not satisfy us. They do not take away our fears, doubts, or insecurities—nor will the latest fashions. But the practice of listening to our inner voice versus the voices that say "Get this, get that gadget and you will be fine." No lies—TRUTH is in one's heart—not out there. Security is not found in things or people—security and safety is found in one's own Self.

Be yourself and listen to your inner voice of God that will guide you. As you sit still in silence, you shall find God—in yourself and in each one of us.

Your love for yourself starts and stops with you.

Let no one bring you down to their level of revenge/retaliation or words that hurt you. Never stoop that low – and may we always look up to others with dignity, admiration and respect. What others say about you is an indication of how they feel themselves. For someone's unkind words show their own sadness and abuse they feel about themselves. Until they notice what they have done, forgive them, bless them, and pray to them. Their hearts are temporarily bruised with anger that comes from deep pain and hurt lying within them. They need your guidance, your prayers, and your forgiveness. They do not need your judgment, criticism, or condemnation. This is not of God—this is their inability to go inside and see "good" while they are going through their own trials and tribulations.

Guidance and love and unconditional love is loving those who have hurt you who you feel are undeserving of your love. You may wish not to see them, yet your relationship lives on with them based on thoughts you think and the words you speak. Thus, if you have nothing good to say—say nothing, for your soul guides you and directs you to whatever you wish to manifest in your thoughts. And in prayer it will manifest based on your thoughts of yourself and that of other friends or foes.

> *Friendship with ourselves*
> *We need to be the bridge*
> *to building profound new relationships*
> *The bridge to helping others*
> *Creates new relationships.*
> *God is inside of you*
> *God is Home.*
> *Your Home is inside of you.*
> *For your heart—this is Home.*

"Heal your past and you have mastered yourself through Love and Forgiveness. Our compassion to ourselves and to others heals our inner world.

That is true success—that is Mastering Thyself"

II

MASTER THYSELF

Life is about making other people happy. We must never harm anyone. We must never give others our hatred or anger. When we do, we must learn where that hurt is coming from so deeply. We must ask ourselves, "Why is it that person allows me this ability to express these negative emotions?" They are present to teach you that you still have so much to learn. We have not learned to master our own actions or behaviors, yet we must learn how we can defend what might need defending.

We must learn not to react to other people's opinions, judgments, or attacks.

How does anyone control their emotions?

Why does one really want to suppress emotion?

Emotions, for all intents and purposes, come from our thoughts; what we think about ourselves expands and becomes our reality. **So what we think about every moment of the day is important—spend as much time in the present as possible.**

Do you know how many thoughts you have in one day? Thoughts create our personal emotions. It is important to believe in what we think and say at all times, every day. The average person has approximately tens of thousands of thoughts each day.

What will slow down our thoughts? Silence.

We breathe in "life" each day. Notice that when you feel blue, you are breathing less effectively. But as soon as you increase your oxygen, you feel rejuvenated. It is so simple. Silence and breathing increase our awareness of the world within us and around us. The law of the universe is applied.

As my Uncle Bruno used to say, focus on giving and exhaling our breath, and the inhaling will automatically take care of itself. Give away your breath, and it will automatically inhale new revitalizing oxygen. The power of breath is one form of mastering yourself.

We need to learn about the importance of breathing in school. We can master ourselves once we master our breath. Breathing helps us get centered and helps us rule our thoughts, mind, and spirit. If you want to be in a better mood—**b-r-e-a-t-h-e.**

Breathe in deeply—share the air—give it away—then take in deeper breaths through your nose.

Awe and bliss become part of our life style when we learn to breathe.

When we breathe through our nose and exhale properly, we give ourselves time to bring oxygen to our blood cells. The rest of our body benefits and, awe and bliss become a way of life. Breathe simply—master yourself by mastering your flow of oxygen through breathing and releasing everything else, including love, giving it back to the earth. Plants do the same. Why not teach your children how to breathe properly.

Why not create the same easy-flow breathing practice. The flow of breath will nurture and cultivate thoughts of love. Thus, in doing so, sooner or later you will have no thoughts but love, and your mind will be in silence due to the concentration of your breath.

Breathe in deeply and exhale completely.

As for meditation, breathing includes exhaling the breath from one's mouth. A simple process, isn't it? Really—try it for a couple of minutes with a few friends. Close your eyes and get one person to time you for one to two minutes and just breathe in silence and see what happens in that minute. What happened?

If you are by yourself, just close your eyes now. Breathe in from your nose and exhale from your mouth. For example, put your two fingers, thumb and index finger, together and sit where you are in a comfortable position for just one minute. Or better still, put your hands in the middle of your chest near your heart and then breathe. When we breathe, we must focus on who we are—do not forget your inner self. Remember that this outer world holds nothing that your inner world wants.

The proper use of breathing is a key to mastering yourself effectively and using breath as a guide to inner growth and expanded consciousness. This creates an inner knowledge of who you really are—in understanding ourselves, we will understand everything else in and around us.

It starts within us:

> *Breathe three times deeply and hold it right down to your stomach. See the difference that breath can do to mastering and knowing yourself. It will help you* **TRUST** *and* **BELIEVE** *in who you really are from a place of inner guidance and personal silence that comes from a love within you that gives you that inner knowing of where you are, who you are, and where you will be in your life starting today. Breathe deeply with love always in mind.*

The next step is to:

Love Yourself Completely as You Really Are

Do you know what smoking is all about? Most people say it relaxes them. Why? Because they are breathing in air, bad air, but nonetheless it is still air. (It can't be as bad as some polluted cities. Thank goodness that is changing now.)

Let's look at this scientifically—what does the power of breath do to our mind and our cells in our body. Let's look at all the aspects of breathing from a medical and scientific perspective!

- ✦ What do you find out about the importance of breath?
- ✦ What cures come out of proper breathing? Are you able to breathe completely every day?
- ✦ What does breathing do to your inner peace?
- ✦ How calm are you in and after your silence?
- ✦ How does that deep breath impact your life and the lives of others?

Mastering ourselves is not mind over matter. It is simply loving life and taking deeper breaths of it. What you breathe in comes back to you. Singing, eating, dancing—any exercise that you love will increase the flow of proper breathing techniques. Try it—breathe properly and see how much better you will heal and feel. Who we think about expands our love or depletes it, depending on what perspective we are coming from—Love, Peace or Anger, Fear, Hatred or Righteousness.

Some people hold on to hate for their lifetime and wonder why they fear to hear the Truth of God waiting within them. They live in their past for they think that is what makes them. Realize that living in the past only takes us away from the power of God within us. What value do we have to share with others when we harbor hate or anger from a deep hurt? Forgiveness leads to growth. Anger or resentment only stifles growth. Once we can look at anger with an observation that says—there goes Peter again—start breathing again.

Holding on to anger does not create inner peace. Ask—when will inner and world peace begin? When we let go of anger. How can we grow in peace if we still harbor anger over anything or anyone?

We learn to master ourselves through the power of our breath (yoga breathing), and asking ourselves the right questions during meditation, prayer, and the reflection of our day. This is the key—for we are getting to know ourselves just a little bit better.

How can we truly master ourselves? When we hold on to guilt, anger or fear, we know that this does not create healing. We create barriers with such negative emotions. Support, rapport, love, and true openness and honesty to ourselves and others comes through teaching only love. Caring, compassion, and understanding ourselves through love helps us all grow.

When we wish to let go of anger or any negative behavior, we must be able to look at it, face it, love it, and say, "I do not want to be this way anymore, God." Then embrace with love our past behavior or our current disappointing behavior.

Breathe in and breathe out, breathe in and breathe out, and thus, we master ourselves. We need to let go and embrace past behavior with love and compassion and forgive ourselves.

> **"We need to Forgive ourselves and ask within us**
> **God to Forgive us; For no one will forgive us until**
> **we first Forgive Ourselves First."**

When we hold on to what has happened and allow it to look us straight in the face and give it "Love and Forgiveness" rather than condemnation, it allows us to grow. How can we grow and be honest with ourselves if we are holding on to anger, shame, fear, or guilt? Only love, acceptance, and compassion can relinquish old patterns, habits that need to be changed—being honest with ourselves with love and inner patience is far more important.

Patience is crucial. In order to master ourselves, we must be willing to be persistent and to persevere and allow ourselves to flow and to grow slowly, rather than quickly. What takes time to learn stays with us much longer. Being kind to ourselves is necessary. When we are hard on others, it is a sure sign of how hard we are on ourselves. The mind plays tricks on us, and we need to be aware that our mind does not control our universe or our inner world. Our mind only categorizes, analyzes, questions, doubts, fears—and is your greatest skeptic. It thinks only of practical and logical answers and constantly questions and labels others and ourselves. Tell me where does this comparing and systemic categorizing get you? Will it bring you any peace, joy, or love? Can it bring you success, health, happiness, wealth, or wisdom? The answer is inevitable—NO! The mind is the devil, the evil and hell that people talk about. Our own minds can either make heaven into hell or hell into heaven. The best thing is to slow down our thoughts and follow God by listening closely to your heart through silence in communication and in communion with God.

Letting go means you will grow.

> *We need to share our time energy, love, communication, commitment, and loyalty.*

God, through the power of our willingness to forgive, leads to mastering ourselves. As we breathe, we feel in our body the power that forgiveness brings—forgiveness transcends all Karma. For all Karma can be transcended through forgiveness. Breathe in forgiveness and see how you have mastered yourself and are prepared to "give thyself" love, peace, and understanding that comes from forgiveness.

> *Say hello to the person beside you,*
> *Tell them your name and introduce yourself.*
> *This is how you spread peace in the world.*
> *As you start with yourself you can give to your-*
> *self and then share that peace with others.*
> *It will manifest itself into Love—pure and*
> *simple.*

III

GIVE THYSELF —

"I may not have a flower to give you, but I offer you this pebble instead."

I might not have a big car to give you, or my house, but I have a couple of bikes for your children. This is a form of showing your love for others and a way of being of service to others. This is learning how to "Give Thyself" by giving to others.

We need to give to ourselves in order to give to others, and we need to give to others in order to give to ourselves. There will always be something for us when we give and when we are thankful for what we are given.

1. **"Take time to breathe deeply"–it is healing–close your eyes.**

You can heal yourself by putting your hands on your heart—or tapping your heart and putting your hands in a position to heal others by healing yourself. **Healing yourself comes from Self-Love and being patient with yourself. A** good indicator of whether we love ourselves can be measured by how much patience we have with ourselves. This includes forgiveness. Once you love yourself, forgiveness is inevitable and very simple.

If you are down at certain times of the day, just lay down on your back, take several minutes to breathe in love, success, and wealth. Breathe self-love back in to your mind and spirit, verbal and nonverbal consciousness, and subconscious.

> **"Let the good and the lovely seep and seed into your subconscious mind every minute of the day…"**

Think about what you learned today! How did you invest your time and energy today? How do you feel about what you learned today? How can you grow for next time and what are you still wishing to work on to be more noble and maintain your level of impeccability.

How can you change if you are unwilling to grow? Change and growth is inevitable, and resistance is natural. Change produces growth, which often projects us into an unknown territory—and we see ourselves—our true selves. Amazingly, we know more about ourselves when we love and care for one another more than ourselves. When we accept ourselves, we accept growth more easily.

2. The Power of Prayer

> *"The power of prayer in itself is a MIRACLE."*
> *What do you think and feel creates your prayer?*
> *Whatever we feel is a prayer. We are prayer—*
> *we need only feel the vibration, "the trembling"*
> *or the goose bumps within us…Prayer impacts*
> *like the ripples from a pebble thrown into the*
> *sea—it impacts every shore line in the world.*
> *The simple effects of prayer can be found in your*
> *thoughts, but especially in your feelings that*
> *come from your heart. Your thoughts can do*
> *nothing, but your mind can move to your heart*
> *to change things in an instant. When one moves*
> *their thoughts from their mind, and instead*
> *are guided by their heart—their feelings—then*
> *one taps into the intuitive power that guides*
> *us all—always. Our heart heals us—masters*
> *us and makes up the five pillars of relation-*
> *ships…beginning with ourselves.*

When we forgive ourselves, ultimately others will forgive us. When we praise ourselves, others will praise us. When we love ourselves and love who we really are, then others will love us…

In judging we take away from our true selves, and it does not lead, most importantly, to forgiveness. Forgiveness comes from the heart, not from the mind. We can transcend even our thoughts by being guided by our hearts, not our minds.

You must first start by not judging others and especially ourselves, How we judge others is a good indication of how we judge ourselves and our lack of forgiving ourselves.

Were you careful with your words today? Where have you grown? What changed in you just by standing and listening to your inner voice today? How did that change you? What did you learn today? How did that create growth in your life today? How did that make you grow—externally or from within?

3. **Love for others.**
   Praying for others.
   Give love to yourself.

Pray for others, and in doing so you release the power within you. When we use our inner power, we gain the love we have to give to ourselves by loving who we are and by giving our prayers to others.

We need to love ourselves and pray for others, especially those you don't like. Saying prayers to people who do not impact your life in any way creates miracles for others and creates fun-filled faith into your own life as well. Try it. It will TRULY CREATE miracles for you. Feel the prayer in your body and truly mean it from your heart. Feel the peace it will create in your body, with your Spirit.

Give thyself—give and live—give, give, give

Silence: Be Still

Listen to Your Heart

1. We are one with all things in this world. We are all part of nature. Spend time with Nature—just sit on the grass.

2. Know yourself by spending time by yourself in pure silence. "The Superior man is always quiet and calm," as Confucius made clear. "In quietness and in confidence shall be your strength." (Isaiah 30:15)

3. Forget your past or future. Be present and just breathe. When you are purely in the "present" moment with God—connected and aligned—you are at Peace, Enlightened, and Happy. It is at these times that you are connected with the Divine residing in each one of us. Forget your past and you will not need to live the past over and over again in your thoughts or behavior. Living in the past causes sadness in one's heart - and living in the future causes anxious feelings.

> **"Fear, anger, and sadness can be transcended through forgiveness."**

You can transcend past fearful experiences and live with new ones that you have created today with present thinking that will bring you love, bliss, peace, and a greater understanding of yourself.

See in your eyes the image of God, Jesus Christ, Buddha, Yogananda, Sai Baba (whatever image best creates a positive role model for you) as you will surely become the archetype you choose to be. Choose wisely. Do your homework/study and listen to your wonderful inner voice. For you know, the person you become is the one you already think you are. You can change this identity by changing your mind as to who you want to be. Be yourself, yet know and be guided by an archetype that you can listen to and who will call upon you and listen to you when you need it most. You will pick up the role and it will become part of you because it is you—you know who you are. You will find it in your willingness to search and seek who you really are inside. God resides in you—

in your heart. Only your ego wishes to distinguish you as separate from everyone and everything. We are all looking for one purpose—to love and be loved.

Serenity comes in our willingness to grow in synergy with one another. We should strive for synthesis rather than creating man-made separations and distinctions. When we make judgments on others, it shows how little we choose to be compassionate and caring for others. Forgive ourselves for that and allow new ways and modes of thinking to seep into and seed your heart and allow your subconscious mind to work for you.

My intention, thought, and prayer is that this book will help you to see things "another" way and develop flexibility to grow and change your life in love, caring, and compassion for yourself and others.

> Living in the Moment
> Loving in the very Moment
> Forgiving oneself will allow others to forgive us.
> Embrace your "mistakes, your "errors of knowledge" and allow it to flow through you and then out of you —
> YOU CAN ONLY, only, only hold onto good once you have embraced your dangers, angers, fearful thoughts, hatred, and allow it to flow through—EMBRACE it will Love—Allow yourself to feel what you feel…
> Embrace it—And then NOW YOU CAN Embrace the New for the old has left your Body and left your consciousness forever and ever—I promise you that it's over.
> Your Ego is Gone, and let it Go—For SPIRIT has taken over you NOW—Love is part of you—for you live with Love within you always and you Give that Love to yourself and all around you—

Unconditional Love Comes when you first give love to yourself.

Follow your dreams and visions to the highest regard— your mission in life is a miracle. Once you have done this with intended action, it is a reality—no longer a vision or a dream, for you are pursuing it with vigor and enthusiasm and allowing the Spirit to work through you to completion.

How do we learn to love? Love is simple. It is not something complicated. It is not even something we need to even study. Love just is—love is just being loved—for love is an energy willingly given by our thoughts and our hearts about ourselves. Self-Love and the love for all others must always come from unconditional love.

What is unconditional love? It is the ability to love someone even when we feel that person is not deserving of our love. Everyone is deserving of our love, and no one ever is excluded. Simply said, love to love and miracles come. Some of us do not believe in miracles—fine—then don't. You can choose what to think, believe, and learn in life. Everyone has the choice to forgive and to love and to expand that love and giving. Anything we give away multiplies, and thus we have more to give.

When we love deeply, we love with a compassion that comes from honesty, truth, and communication.

"Love, Peace, and Understanding creates more love in our lives." (Lama Margaret)

As we give, we find that we have even more to give to others. As we live, we find we are in **even deeper** than deep, in our love for others and ourselves.

We love people—we love openly and we give openly. We share lots, and we give lots to ourselves. As we give, we have even more to give to ourselves and to others. It is by giving our self-nurturing "Self" and pampering ourselves we learn the essence of love. Nurture yourself with Self-Love. This will expand to even more Self-Love. This is the key to even more Self-Love. For happy is he who loves himself! Now we have Love to give to ourselves and to others.

If we care for just one person in this world, there will be no more lonely people in the world. This is a fundamental principle.

**Cultivating love starts by loving those
you do not like.**

Love is simple—simple—simple!

**"To get wisdom is to love oneself; to keep under-
standing is to prosper."**

(Proverb 19:18)

Know it—you'll see it
Believe it—and It will come!

In Spirit we grow, in flesh we flow
Combine them together and we maintain balance in
Spirit and on Earth
We are One with God

Guilt–Mistakes

Guilt of one's mistakes gets us nowhere. Relinquish your doubt for what has happened. Let it go and be willing to understand why we feel guilt. It is a wasted emotion when we hold on to past mistakes for too long rather than learning the lesson and moving forward to the next mark in our lives—called the present—now—today!

Believe in thyself
Believe in God
Believe in Nature
Believe in ourselves.

We sometimes need objects such as beads to help us believe in ourselves. We need beads because we are having a hard time believing in ourselves. The beads won't change us, but they will surely soothe us, allowing us to be quiet, be silent, and to love ourselves. Loving ourselves and believing in ourselves, involving communication of any form, is important. As we share and become more loving to ourselves, we can give to others. In giving we learn to forgive. When we feel we cannot forgive, we need to remember that any one with discipline knows we can do anything and change anything in our lives. It is up to us "for all things are possible with God."

Trust your voice—trusting your intuition means being able to go within and listen to your voice. Love within ourselves is the greatest love of all. Peter wants you to know that he loves you dearly.

Believe in Thyself. Believe and visualize where you want to be, not where you are now. Fake it until you make it—this really works.

+ When you put two people together who Love one another, you become three.

+ Your past is always over.

Let go of the past and let God take care of the details... don't talk about the past. Place your attention in God, which is everywhere within you.

When you talk about the past, you sometimes need to live this story in the present. Why destroy your present moment with the past? You are only dividing your energies, and it will only divide you more. Forget the past or the future.

Think of the new and create today as if you were creating for five centuries from now—think long term when building. What do you do when you live in the present moment—you live with God. It is in each of us to live in the moment—and give to others.

5. Be here in this present moment—called now!

Calmness comes when we find God within us, as well as in the flowers we plant, in the roses we give, in the tulips we pluck, in the cherry blossoms we admire—smell flowers—talk with Nature—listen to ourselves.

Hug humanity—lend one's hand—to love all others, knowing in lending we are truly giving of ourselves from the heart of God in us. But how can we love another person until we forgive and Pamper ourselves. Be yourself and love who you are—others will love you.

It has been scientifically proven that 7 to 12 hugs a day can increase your hemoglobin levels. Touch is important. Tell me, if a baby is crying, what will soothe him/her? "Here, honey baby, here is a tissue for you. Wipe your tears!" (Think about it—this is what we do to adults.) We love from within, and with that love we give life to all around us and especially ourselves.

We give as we take in the sweet fresh air of the sun, moon, and star-lit sky that is looking down upon us. In those stars are our dreams. We need to direct our emotions toward our long-range purpose or personal dream. In doing so, we become close to God or, mildly put, we get in touch with our inner world. We get to touch upon divine love and light within us. We get to know who we are, and we get to share that with God who dwells within us. If we remember the importance of giving in to our desires, life will be full of more love. Desires are not evil or bad. They are the essence of life that makes us grow and propels and prepares us for the next level of our dreams. We can put these into action by owning our true desires. Action can include silence and inaction, for even in inaction we are processing our inner guidance for the action we will need to proceed.

How do we do this?

1. Through creating new habits over 30 days.
2. By reading your plans to your subconscious mind every morning when you awake and every evening when you go to sleep. Write your written desires and achieve them by giving them back for your subconscious mind to process throughout the evening, and then God will guide you to what to put into action in the morning. **Trust in yourself and believe and know you will receive that answer.** When you believe, answers appear in ways you can't imagine— in dreams, visions, words, or through answers given through others. "The Voice" will mean something to you and will guide you to where you need to go.
3. Simply taking time to listen.

Go within and take time to listen: "BREATHE,"
"Breathe" and "Breathe" and "Breathe." The answer is in the air.

We need to be willing to make gradual changes every day. Where do we put our attention? We become what we put our attention on. What thoughts do we think about ourselves and others. What kind of questions do we ask ourselves during the day—morning, afternoon, and night. Where have we invested our energy today? Are we thinking and feeling with love and faith or are we investing our energy on negativity, anger, anxiety, or fears? Where is this anxiety coming from? Why are we anxious versus caring and compassionate? Are we looking too much at ourselves and not enough at others? We're learning about showing and giving by doing just that. Giving unconditional love to everything and everyone in our thoughts, minds, and hearts always. What kinds of questions do we ask ourselves at night? For we are all here for each other…always…

I am here with you always—the Spirit can and will connect. Know that you have the power to move mountains and clouds. Our consciousness affects the environment—give the world and the people in this world your love—give it away to everyone.

Life is about giving, and giving is also present in the process of forgiving. Giving unconditionally is a selfless and generous way to give. It brings us peace and helps us succeed by learning to give unconditionally anyway—no matter what the circumstances are. This is a serene and successful way to be because you maintain your peace. By giving generously with unconditional love first and foremost for ourselves and then to all others, we are better able to give to all humanity.

As we forgive ourselves, we are able to give to others. However, giving to receive what we feel we deserve is wrongful thinking. **We must give in order to see how much giving transforms us** and others into well inspired/transformed and spiritual beings.

Give generously and you will always have much more to give. You will have even more to give than you thought possible. Actually, you will be able to give even more than you have ever imagined. It might even amaze you that you have so much to give from your Heart—but when the giving comes from our "Heart," then this giving is infinitely abundant and inexhaustible. Again, for it comes from our Heart, not our egotism. Giving creates peace.

Love transforms through giving—To ourselves and then to all others

We must learn how to give, and the true essence of giving is to love whatever you wish to transpire. "Give with love always in mind" for love comes from within us. It is a heart space versus an intellectual mind consciousness. Some of us think our consciousness starts with our minds, but this is not true. It starts with our inner and invisible Self that comes from within and works with our honest heart space. It is the only space that gives life and creates life. Any other form is only an illusion we have created in our minds. **We have created in our minds what we choose to cultivate.**

When we create time to nurture ourselves with love, then we are taking care of ourselves. A good indication of not taking care of ourselves is our negative behaviors and thoughts. We can reverse this easily by nurturing our true Self. For example, through the power of meditation and breath, we can slow physical time into infinite time that will heal our consciousness and reduce the illusion of stress, anxiety, and fears that do not exist.

The healing power of humanity comes from presenting Love to all; for love is all we ever need to give to the world around us and especially within us. Love starts with ourselves—that's infinite.

When we are able to pursue time to nurture ourselves to love infinite space that brings us peace, we are able to give from that wealth of infinite abundance. This creates a positive flow of healthy energy that is not based on human time, but is based on God's time. We are then able to allow things to flow, and the healing force of humanity presents itself with love, for love is all we ever need to give.

And the love that starts with ourselves and this infinite energy will generate more peace for all the people around us. They will feel our peace based on how much time we've taken to nurture ourselves with this infinite space we call love. Although love seems like a gushy word, it is in giving to ourselves that we're able to give and generate that same peace to those around us. This is why it's important to understand that peace starts in our own living room and not on holidays and getaways.

> *Love is not something you can hoard or hold*
> *on to Like some kind of possession—a mistake*
> *made all too often Love is something you give*
> *away to others. Love is not exclusive—it does*
> *not make one special or another more special.*
> *Love does not divide, conquer, or exclude*
> *anyone. It embraces change and grows with*
> *differences. It is in these times that we unite, but*
> *maintain our uniqueness.*
>
> *Grow and guide through synergy and see all*
> *the commonalities people really do share In this*
> *sharing we become wiser in our knowledge and*
> *love for others. We give each other pieces of our*
> *wisdom through giving. Excitement comes in*
> *giving at all times—for there is love. One must*
> *love thyself before you can offer anything to*
> *anyone. We need to know love from within and*
> *then share it with others.*
>
> *All we need to do is look within for the divine*
> *and feel God's guidance. Know God helps you*
> *to breathe—you don't even need to try. Just be*
> *conscious of your breathing and see how much*

> *love you give to yourself, then share it generously*
> *with everybody in prayer and with all whom*
> *you come in contact. Especially remember those*
> *in your heart you do not know—give away*
> *your love to everyone—pray and visualize*
> *peace—leave no one behind. Practice breathing*
> *properly. Learn to connect with your internal*
> *God and work toward creating peace in your*
> *world.*

To experience a fulfilling life, we must be willing to love and care with compassion. This leads to ultimate happiness. Show your weak points and grow from your shadow—your dark side has the most to reveal to you and share it only with those you can trust. Go within and examine yourself with the right questions. Always ask yourself questions that will empower you.

What did I learn today?
How have I grown?
Where have I invested my thoughts?
Was I kind to myself and others?
How can I improve my smile?
How have I improved my loving, kindness,
compassion, and caring for others?
Am I living my life based on peace…
that will bring me joy?

In the evening ask yourself whose lives have I impacted today and how did it change us both? Send love to those people you are having a tough time with and pray to them. Write a letter stamped with love and compassion and a willingness to reconcile your strained relationship. Ask yourself, "What have I learned today that I did not know yesterday?" Sit silently for a while and listen to the peaceful and practical answers.

> Seed only the good
> May God fly by your feet
> Trickle through your toes
> And you will find love
> Where everybody goes

Happiness comes in caring for others.
Bring peace to the family—by finding Peace in yourself.
Listen to what other people feel—truly listen and care.

Remember to go slowly in the tunnel. The analogy I like to use is the train going through the tunnel. As you slow the train down, be in your emotion. Allow room to grow and be in your feelings before you let it go gently to a new profound thought pattern. Then you will see the light…at the end of the tunnel.

When you embrace whatever you are going through, when you face up to your past—you allow yourself to grow.

**Nothing you face can ever control you—
"close the door to the past."**

Embrace whatever you are going through. **When you face it,** your past or present moment will never control you. Control comes from holding onto the present challenges or past mistakes. It is folly to think that your present or past mistakes are mistakes. No—let them go. Admit your faults and then move on. Guilt and shame are a waste of time. This is valuable energy that needs to be directed toward higher levels of consciousness based on love, joy, forgiveness, and a willingness to grow.

SILENCE

Peace equals Silence

Silence is love and love is Silence. Peace comes in Silence. Love grows with Silence. God is Silence and love is Silence within our own hearts. As we give, we will find we have even more to give to ourselves and others. As we open our hearts, we find peace in our Spirit, and it is in this that we love.

It is in this peace that we grow—and it is in this peace that we find spiritual sustenance to love others. Kindness comes when we find ways to spend our time in Silence. It is in Silence that we grow—letting go of our desire to be right, we grow.

In silence and in peace—we let go of our personal identities, realign, and connect with our inner wisdom and know we are one with God.

Thus, love will appear again in our lives. With the embracing of the shadow, we will see the light and unconditional love. Thus, Silence equals PEACE. We grow in LOVE.

Psychology alone without love expression leaves no room to grow and no room to release the heart from its chains and bars to inner-personal growth. Love comes with feelings. Ego goes only with thought and calculating one's next move. Where is Peace in that? Only love guides us to wisdom.

Psychology alone does "nothing" for anyone. Knowledge without spirituality is just wasted knowledge.

Light House

There is the light of love that awaits within us. There is no other power more appealing than love. Love heals all things completely.

Without love you cannot gain wisdom.

Love equals wisdom.

For love is energy.

Knowledge will not gain you Wisdom. Only love can bring you closer to understanding knowledge; love equates to wisdom.

You cannot love humanity if you hate others. Embrace your hate, understand it, then toss the hat of hatred gently down the stairs and say good-bye to it—and choose to love again, like a child once inside of you.

Can you be of God or experience like qualities if you hate other people in your heart? Animosity and anger are different. With anger we are dealing with injustice. We are dealing with hurt feelings. Hate, which is a very strong word, should be avoided and eliminated from our vocabulary.

Consider the following:

+ an ethical and compassionate life—where we forgive ourselves and others, acts of loving kindness, and
+ be in God's presence by helping others, and together love ourselves and others.
+ talk to God through prayer (i.e., words of Psalms), perform spiritual practices. Listen to God by breathing in love and giving thyself love, then exhaling to give love away.
+ Meditation has a profound impact on our lives. Read inspiring literature, listen to your inner voice.
+ Ask questions out loud and listen to the voice in your head and the calmness and peace in your heart. When

you feel peace, then you know you have connected with God. God comes from the heart and never from the head.

What you are is what you see and put in your mind and heart on a daily basis. Relationships require us to love, to give, to be open, and to love when it is most difficult. We need to give when we do not want to, when we feel that person does not earn it or even expect it. Yet as we grow, we learn that there is no one who does not require our love. We all need to love and be loved. It is only when we love that we know the true essence of our own lives, to give love and send love to all.

We are here to care for one another and share in each other's lives—love, happiness, joy, and bliss, even if we also are feeling anguish, anger, suffering, or pain. Together we must care and together we must love and help one another and see within us all the commonalities that we truly share. In essence, once you love who you are, you have everything.

**"Secure me with my thoughts and feelings,
O Lord, for they become my prayers"**

To integrity and compassion
For one another's needs, wants, and desires
Help one another enthusiastically
Achieve our desires, visions, dreams, goals, and Purpose, in
each one of our lives.

We are here for each other—to care for one another.

And to give to one another—"forgiveness."

A Technique to "Forgive Thyself"

Holding on to anger or resentment is a sign of low self-esteem. Forgiveness is natural and simple—yet initially it seems like a very difficult thing to do. Try just forgiving yourself—look in the mirror and truly mean it from your heart.

What do you mean from your heart? Say it loudly and clearly while looking in the mirror and say **"God forgive me."** I want to forgive myself for any harm or any mistakes that I have made. Please forgive me and help me move forward to being a better person. While doing this—put and place your hand, or both hands, on your heart clutched as a fist or flat. It doesn't matter—all that matters is that you feel your heart. Touch your heart so your heart knows and feels you are speaking from your heart—not from your head.

Focus on Forgiveness
And
Align yourself With Forgiveness

Day by day

It will come and
Become part of you.
It is used all day until the day comes that we no longer judge
or condemn others,
That is when forgiveness will no longer be necessary.
When we never judge or condemn anyone—this is when
forgiveness will no longer be necessary.

May we all love one another equally -from our heart—never from our minds that creates judgments.

What creates judgments creates turmoil in our bodies— what heals us is never our minds - but our hearts.

Our bodies create judgments

Our mind calculates and organizes things into neat compartmentalized "areas" that generalizes.

Words are based on logic and reasoning that leads to "illogical" answers to very "simple solutions."

IV

LOVE THYSELF

"Our main purpose in life is to help each other grow, to love and care for one another in kindness and compassion.

Forgiveness always comes when we love."

We will always find what we are looking for. Anger will fester in one's own self. Hate is directed at, leading to destruction. Anger toward others is a sign of anger that one has for one's self. Anger comes from deep hurts or an injustice.

We change others with our compassionate hearts. With physical force or anger, control works little magic. It only leads to more violence. It is our compassion, our tender and caring hearts that turn others to us. Our love transforms others with the power of intent to be who we really are within and in return others turn to themselves and their true inner Self.

Love who you really are by going within.
We need to love who we are…
For in doing so—in loving ourselves—we grow.

When we avoid changing others, we grow ourselves. Mature love comes from working with ourselves. How are we going to grow? How are we going to invest our energy, time, and thoughts? Are we growing emotionally? Are we learning from our actions today? Focus on today, and where we want to be! How do we choose to grow? Are we happy where we are? Are we looking to change by looking at changing circumstances or by changing ourselves or others? Our circumstances are created by ourselves—we need to change our own vibrational connections to our words that come from the Spirit to change our desired outcome. The outcome flows as we flow, with no other objective than loving, caring, and understanding one another with compassion and forbearance. If our words do not condemn, there will be no need for forgiveness. Know we are all one with the Spirit.

Oneness is created from the Spirit—
that creates all things, becomes all things and
is all things—all at the same time
The Spirit is responsible for all that exists—
from creating a tree to providing water
and all its other needs.
It is all one—and it is all protected.

When we have self-love, we allow only love to enter our

hearts. Our integrity and self-love will prevent others bringing us down.

Laughter is important, and dancing 20 minutes a day is important to build lasting relationships with one another, with a loved one, a couple, et cetera. Hugs are very important as is touch, which brings us alive. Hugging increases our hemoglobin in our body. Remember, laugh a lot, for it heals our spirit-soul.

"The Healing Power of Laughter"

Solution is to Laugh Lots. It will Heal You.

1. Laugh at yourself—it heals your Spirit.
2. The healing power of laughter will transform you and the people around you—the Love and Smile of a friend, mother-father, or stranger Truly heals our Soul-Spirit—And helps us to maintain our "Spirit" of enthusiasm in our lives.
3. Love Creates Healing.
   Love Brings Healing.
   Love Is Healing.
4. When you love yourself, you grow.
5. Patience shows you have Self-Love.

Isabella knew how to live her life to the fullest, but she attributes that to trial and error as well as love. But hers was a life of teaching only LOVE. So if you are going to make mistakes in love—make big mistakes and learn from them.

At least you can say you loved, rather than not loved others and yourself. It is in love that we acquire wisdom. Many believe we acquire knowledge and wisdom and then gain the meaning and understanding of love. Give away love, and you will always have more to give away.

Friends believe in you and your dreams,
love you when you are down,
care for you when you are sick,
cherish you when you don't love yourself.
These are some of the signs of TRUE friendship.

Friends love you when you are strong and are there for you when you need them. They build you up—when you least expect it. They are the ones who know you well enough to see you through your challenges rather than try to see through you!

Work to building a better relationship with others by building a good relationship with yourself, for how you treat others is a good indication of how you treat yourself.

God provides all that we need in divine order.

Believing is yourself is knowing who you are, loving who you are, and where you want to go in your venture in life. Give as much as you can, and you will always have more to give. Be who you want to be and see yourself grow internally. Shout from a mountain top and listen to the voice repeat itself. Whatever you gave is what nature will give back to you.

> Seed only good thoughts
> Seed only good prayers
> Seed only good love for it is the love
> you will ever pray for.
> Unconditional love versus conditional love
> will make or break your day
> Choose always to love one another.

Give in to kindness, compassion, and ethical living. Stay away from rules that direct you away from love. Live by principles, not rules to create peace in your lives. Love will bring far more greater rewards than any other thing. Give what you want and you will always find more to give, for love is equal to God. It is infinite, and love is boundless energy with no time strap around it. It is the universal cosmic energy that flows through us all and gives to us all—UNCONDITIONALLY.

Love is the healer, not time. Our Heart, Soul, or Spirit heals our wounds—not time or intellectual thoughts. Thoughts can be our gateway into heaven or our prison into hell. Destructive thoughts are our own doing. These must be mastered and relinquished and be aware of the destruction they do to our minds, hearts, and bodies.

Loving ourselves creates an energy to give our body the healing it needs. Nothing matters more than taking care of ourselves. You must love yourself first before you can love your neighbor. Love who you are and where you are in your life, and all else will cease to matter.

For happy is he who loves himself.

Give from the wealth of abundance we call Life. The more we give to others, the more life gives willingly to us—Peace, Harmony, and Tranquility. Love will continue to expand our Spirits and minds. Yet love is not a thought—love is not even a feeling. It is a mighty energy—an invisible power that gives us our Life. The more we give love away, the more love we have to give away. And I repeat this principle over and over again to impress upon you how important it is to give love.

Talk less, listen more, eat less, and share more. There is always more to give and more to share. Remember what our parents told us to do—it is important to share with others. The more we share, the more it shows that we care.

Master your own destiny by knowing first who you are. Giving thyself means forgiving thyself. Embrace your circumstances. Embrace your sorrow, challenges, anger, insecurities, and frustrations. When you embrace sorrow, do not minimize it by telling someone to get "over it."

Everyone must embrace their pain. Allow yourself to go

through the "tunnel" like a locomotive, and at the end of the tunnel you will see the light. We can only give once we have love and forgiveness for ourselves.

Love others as well as you love yourself—what you give comes from what you have inside of you. For in loving ourselves—love will appear in others—happy is he who loves himself.

Let your weakness become your strength
For it is in these times that
we are growing that we learn the most
For what you need to learn the most—
you can teach the best!

We all know what is faster than Sound—**LIGHT!**

Do you know what is faster than Light—**THOUGHT!**

Emotions are created by thoughts. This means we can change our emotions by purely changing our thoughts. So be careful what you think—and truly listen to your intuition or thoughts. They will guide and tell you what to do.

Next—our thoughts come from **out-there**. But it is important that the answer comes from within—like a buzzing bee, we can scan the thoughts which divide us.

We were brought to this world to love one another.

What you love will surely love you.

What you don't like won't like you.

It's up to you to love and it's up to you to rid yourself of the clutches of evil or devilish thoughts that transpire from repetitive negative thinking: Negative thinking comes from an inability to love and care for ourselves and one another.

Judging versus Acceptance

Envy–Hate–Anger–Jealousy–Greed–Doubt - and the list goes on.

Do not resist–accept change and grow by loving yourself.

Cultivate thoughts and feelings of love, compassion, equanimity, forgiveness for others and yourself. Make this a daily habit and USE such words and repeat them five to ten minutes and see the difference it will make in your own life and especially in the lives of others.

Love is compassion—it is the richest of all riches. It completes you and holds you with open arms, preparing you to share and to give with honesty. Sincerity is an energy that heals. In fact, love is from the heart of the Universe. There is no energy that can be as successfully revealing as love—it is the only healing force in the Universe and withstands all hardships and forgives all forms of errors with compassion and understanding even at the worst of times.

Love is unconditional and it is what you need to give to yourself every day.

When you learn with love, you also heal with love. Only with love do you see the TRUE acts of kindness and most of the true actions of visible and invisible miracles.

Kind words create miracles. Remember that. Kind words really do create miracles. You get what you give. The power is enormous—it withstands all things. And when all else has fallen by the wayside, "Love still stands."

Love—how do you get it? Just be love. Loving yourself is as good or better than any other intoxication for at least it heals the Soul and body from all forms of ailments. Pay attention to where your body is hurting. Know those are only temporary bruises. Love heals all. No one is excluded from this innate power, and that means no one. Love is equal to all and healing to all. Only man's mind has created distinctions and separations with labels and categories to feel superior or inferior to others. However, it is these attitudes that also bring about the largest and fiercest wars of mankind. Everyone is equal—no one is better than anyone else. Love yourself by building your own self-esteem and self-worth. Choose to be at peace with yourself by connecting with the loving One within you.

Misery—what does misery need—COMPANY. Anyone who feels superior or inferior to another is insecure. Pure and simple. It is from these insecurities and fears emanating from our egos versus **our hearts full of love**, which makes war inside ourselves, and it takes us away from our PEACE.

Peace is the ultimate goal for you will Love. When we are at PEACE with ourselves, we love ourselves and who we really are. How can we help one another and make each other happy and at peace? **"Peace" starts in our own living rooms.**

Who are we? We are not our nationalities—for this weakens us and creates distinctions that only separate us. We are all one in this humanity called "Life." in giving love, you will find **"the more you give, the more it expands."**

What can be more powerful than the love of a mother? God's love! In our mother's and father's love lies the greatest love of all. The love that God has for us. For we are all images of God, and we are God when we align ourselves from within. We are capable of creating and manifesting miracles with the power of our subconscious mind and the power of the internal love that we have.

"Love one another by first loving yourself."

Be kind to yourself—be gentle. Be tender and venture in Life in a carefree manner, allowing purity of Spirit to flow through you and in you. Go in true peace and serenity and love one another. Love is special when it comes from the heart...for it is the only true place where it can come from.

Ethical living comes from within us—when someone says "I'm proud of you," it doesn't mean it is love because love is different from pride. Pride is not love energy as love heals, love forgives, love does not condemn. The opposite of love is fear and not hate and the opposite of pride is shame. Both are not significantly empowering emotions or thoughts.

"Love does not condemn, so it need not forgive".

When our mother says "I'm so proud of you," remember this is not love. All mothers and fathers have the capacity to use their hearts and minds at higher levels of energy than just pride for their children. Life is not competition as much as cooperation and interdependence in relationships with others, teams, and groups.

> **"It is about building relationships**
> **We must build relationships with others**
> **Not destroy them…"**

We are one and in love we must share in each other's roles to secure and help one another grow in self-love and self-worth through healthy positive self-image of ourselves and the people around us—for we are all made in the image of God.

"Love Thyself and Trust Thyself–that we are all one with God - within us all–"

The Root to Cultivating Love

How can we love each other?
What is the root to loving one another?

To love the ones we like or love?
Yes, that is part of Love.
If one wants to cultivate Love, one must and
needs to Love those you do not like,
That is the root or the purpose of LOVE.

Life in its essence is loving one another—and giving to others our self-worth and love that emanates within us all. Life is truly about giving. For "when we Love ourselves, we Love our world…"

"Anything is possible when we believe and trust ourselves.

We easily embrace things new when we believe and trust in ourselves…and follow what you know and not what others tell you to be true."

V

TRUST THYSELF
TRUST YOURSELF

"Believing in yourself to know you
CAN Do Anything…
with God…
with God's guidance
from within."

"Trust your intuition by Listening to your
Heart,
Not your mind."

Trust your intuition.

I want Peace—
Peace comes through meditation
In one-Self–true-Self
In doubting and questioning that which is not TRUE –thus
believing in thyself.

You will see it when you visualize it
with all your heart—with all your Soul
And truly start believing in yourself
knowing you are honoring yourself.
I will exalt you
With honor, glory, and praise.

Please maintain your humbleness -
it is your key to successful living.
Get your creative juices flowing
now and every day.

An acknowledgment to Isabella
Thank you—you've awakened my SOUL

Acknowledge your own Divinity.
Be thankful.
For when you know your own Enlightenment
and Divinity within,
You are more able to spread peace from within
and to all.

TRUST

Your
intuition

by
Listening
to
Your
"Heart,"
not
Your
MIND.

**Know your own infinity to do and change
anything in your world...**

Trust in yourself. Trust that which is not seen and that that which is not heard from others, but rather trust that which has been heard through yourself. If God be for you, who can be against you when you have the eternal God within you. Trust in yourself by being your own best friend. Nurture yourself and trust your God given abilities—your intuition. God guides you and protects you wherever you go. Trust in God—trust yourself as God trusts you. Believe in yourself. God trusts and guides you—all in divine order.

Believe in yourself and your abilities. Find out what those innate abilities are. Breathe a few moments and ask God what are truly my abilities. Ask others and listen quietly for the response will come.

Believing in ourselves means listening to our intuition.

Believing in ourselves—believing in our intuition—

means our ability to listen to our hearts and the little voice in our head. Someone who wishes for you not to listen to your instincts will tell you "What? You're hearing voices—go see a psychiatrist—you're going nuts." Funny, but when we listen to our intuition, it works. When we ignore it, it hurts—why? When we go beyond what the inner world of our Universe says is best for us to do, we Trust Thyself. Our mind is logical, reasonable, and intellectual—but trusting in yourself does not come from the brain—it comes from your heart.

The outer world is like the atom that is negative from the outside periphery. In the center, within each of us, is the positive force. That positive force is our hearts, and we must listen to that voice in silence and not to the voice ahead, behind, or in front of us. Instead, let us have the power to listen and breathe and go within to know the wisest answers to all of our divinely guided answers awaiting within us. We need to listen closely to our INTUITION and hear it once again.

When love prevails, nothing else matters… Love makes all things possible–for in God's love and in love there is peace, forgiveness, equanimity - divine unconditional love

We are all one, meaning coming from having faith in ourselves.

Self-confidence is just that—FAITH. When anyone takes our self-confidence, self-love, self-worth, self-esteem, they are in need of help themselves. Only with love can you let them find themselves—trust that you are able to help your friends. True friends focus on what a wonderful person you really are.

Friends increase your self-worth—they do not compete with you, they guide you, care for you, listen to you, and love you for who you are and who you are becoming. Friends don't bring you down or criticize you—don't do it to yourself either. They trust your judgment and genuinely want to see only your deepest desires come true. Why? For they care and bring out the best in you—as well as reveal anything that needs to be learned. Friends always stand by your side. Be your own best friend and stand by your own side and listen to the answers that come to you. Make decisions based on choices within your own inner guidance. Ask for the inner guidance to help you find the answers that will help guide you to the light and your journey's destination.

Friends see only what's possible. They look at all the obstacles, yet see only the opportunities. They see only what they know you can do—your own inner strength—God's strength—together you have synergy.

Hate is not of God. The opposite of love is more than hate, but fear stemming from hate—so avoid using that word. When we replace hate, jealousy, envy, or resentment from our minds and fill our hearts with forgiveness and unconditional love, we will see that all things are possible with love in our hearts and God to follow. Trust that your heart will guide you to where you need to go—all in divine order.

Faith infinitely moves mountains—which means you trust yourself. When you have faith—trust—in which something you still have not seen, you are trusting in yourself to visualize what you want to see…you see-visualize and believe in yourself—this trust is deep rooted from within. When you know and trust the infinite divine within, you can create peace all around you.

Trust in the infinite God within you to create miracles in you and your world.

Now, with a deep breath and in great contemplation and visualization of what you want in life—you have mastered thyself by listening and seeing what you need. By first going within—the guiding inner power and inner voice—your intuition from your heart—that lets you know what to do next.

When you know thyself, you trust thyself.

When you love yourself, you will give of thyself—

When you believe in yourself, you will trust the intuition that is your infinite divine self guiding you to where you need to go and where you need to be—right now—

I love you—trust yourself to know you are divinely guided, and with this power know you can do anything you want to achieve in your life. It is so wonderful to wake up with a purpose every morning.

Pray this affirmation—every day

*"I am infinite and divinely guided. God is me.
I choose to align myself and tap into what
is the inner strength and peace that God
within me provides. It is given to me in
abundance—love, health, peace, success,
and wealth. I pray and visualize peace, love,
caring, and compassion in the world. I feel
it in my body, and I am now complete."*

Always build yourself up—**TRUST THYSELF**—never
question your own ability. Build your Spirit every
day, and you will know you can do anything.

AFTERWORD

**"Remember Something Good is Going to Come
out of this"**
**God's Abundance is Flowing in Everyone's Lives
All IN Divine Order**

Who Does This Belong To?

Are you feeling some pain in your body or anger and a headache? Ask yourself "Who does this belong to?" allow yourself to heal your own body, and know you can be your own best friend. "Physician Heal Thyself"

How Can It Get Better Than This.

Ask yourself Everyday and in every hour of your day: "How can it get better then this." And it will, just watch how it will get better then this~ see what happens when you just deliver these powerful words to your heart~

Thankful Every Morning
**God's Abundance is flowing through me every
moment of the day.**

**And the God Within will take care of ALL
THINGS everything all in Divine Order.
With Much Love To you All, I love you,**

PETER SAMMARCO

Contact us for any products, services, or 'relationship building':

www. FivePillars.ca
www.HealYourself.ca
Telephone 250-382-9397

ACKNOWLEDGEMENTS

Be thankful for everything in life as it's far more important than success. Being thankful in advance of one's success is true success. Peter wishes to acknowledge the following individuals who have been the impetus to beginning this book and who contributed in so many ways. He wishes to express his heartfelt gratitude.

Thanking our Infinite Creator, eternal within us all, for writing this very book.

To My MOTHER and FATHER: You have been there to Guide your children with love, care ~ compassion, open communication, and always teaching we can do anything and seeding self-confidence in all ways, from asking Isabella and me to memorize a poem in five to ten minutes to talking about our day and asking us what we learned today; and you show your love with God's love in your heart at all times. Your wisdom is Deep and your genius ways incredible and a delight to all that you have helped along the way. Everyone who has stayed in your home has benefited by your Love. You care so much for everyone in this world. I know, DAD, you have been able to help so many friends and love to be there for anyone who asks. You are really the Man who says Ask and you shall receive. Outside of meditation, just your presence alone really moves mountains. You are always speaking from God in our heart, and you always make sense with your words because your stories are of God in you directing your every word, creating Peace to all who are in your presence. Also, your amazing direction helps so many around us. You are truly also a Genius engineer and carpenter who loves to make other people's lives happy. Your most important client, I know being Sara, shows how Spirit really moves you and lives through you in your heart and eyes and touch of love at all times in your smile! I love you, DAD. MOM: You are simply the Best Mother anyone can have. You have done many things that show your care for humanity. Feeding birds from your hands is great, but your love for your family even greater. Your constant loyalty, hard-working nature, and commitment through thick and thin is even more amazing than anything else. Your own Self Love shows in your patience with your loved ones, and, as usual, with your BOYS. I love you for your drive and commitment to learn, and you always have answers to simply great solutions that no one even thinks about. Pat and Sara Sammarco, the most amazing parents one can ever have -- Peter's parents -- who taught him to have practical common sense through life and who speak with openness, truth, and wisdom and live with unconditional love. Your

Love and Support is immensely Important. YOU ARE BOTH So Amazing ~ and ALWAYS LOVED~.

"Seed the good and the good shall follow."

Lama Margaret — your consistent unconditional support, love, and understanding is incredible. With you in Peter's life everything has been made possible. You have taught so many how to get close to God. The world is a better place with you in it. I am thankful for your friendship. Peter loves you dearly.

Isabella Maria Sammarco — Peter's sister, who is his friend and inspiration. (You have awakened Peter's soul.) You continually guide and Keep Me to Myself. You have always Been there for ME, and you are More alive today than ever Before. We both knew the last time our eyes met before the paramedics took you away from the house would be the last time our eyes would meet, but we also know we have been there for each other. As you used to say, there are three people that are most important in this world: me, myself, and I. I love you and miss your human presence still to this day ~ we will see you soon. You are really someone who I will always love so dearly in my heart. No one can compare to the love we have for each other.

Edward Gibney — who is a guide, friend, and unequivocal inspiration. Your music lives on for you teach more than just music. You Truly do Teach "A Prelude To Brass Playing" while walking your Talk! We both truly love our conversations together over dinner. Thank you so much my Dear Friend. We have achieved so much together; and you are an inspiration for so many in the field of health and music; but even more important things, in love and friendship you lead the pack, and have done so much!

To all of Peter's spiritual teachers and guidance from friends of all spiritual and religious faiths — "I know in the end we are all one with God" — and knowing is far more important than all our beliefs. Peter thanks you all for following and allowing him to follow his inner knowing, beyond thought, transcending the mind, and following that inner voice that resides in our hearts.

Kinoe Oates — for her inspiration and her Samurai guidance. "Do it now, do it today." You are more than just a friend, Kinoe — "Ti Amo! Ti Voglio Bene, Bella." You are a very important Part of my life. Kinoe~san, you have helped in so many numerous ways that I am indebted for life. I am eternally grateful and enjoy your company immensely. We Truly understand each other. All of your graphic design-writer help and your eye for colors and love for detail has helped so much in the process of making this very book. You are always there for Peter and always teaching to love and forgive your parents as well as maintaining many ways of the Samurai, including the mastering of all areas in your life. You have taught invaluable lessons that are shared between each other's hearts. You bring peace in People's world with your Love: That is your

Mastered and valued Samurai principles of Wisdom. You make others feel good.

James Roberts, who taught religious studies with spiritual confidence and faith with passion, allowing us to grow to our fullest potential by following our inner voice, and knowing this to be true. Peter is deeply thankful. Your time and effort was teaching him that his inner voice was actually God talking to him — our intuition — and following through with our intuition. You are truly Amazing James and have made such a definite infinite Difference in Peter's world and those in your classand around you! You are truly loved, cherished, respected, and admired deeply ~ I am so thankful for your presence in everyone's world.

Dorothy and Bruno, you introduced us to so many spiritual authors, including Mr. Thomson's and many friends, as well as other important Sages and Teachers who lived from a place of Great importance: ~The God Within. Also, books on the importance of the changing cells in our bodies and the power that we can learn from these wonderful writers of Genius.

I Wish I could say this shorter than this, but I am finding that you both were so important in our child-rearing years moving to West Vancouver from Montreal. You taught us only love and gave us a tremendous amount of love. Your presence and love was all we ever needed in our world. In our world nothing ever went wrong because you both were in it, helping to share the importance of the invisible Self and how we can heal our body and become completely transformed spiritual beings when we transcend the mind and body and relinquish hate and judgments and live from that place of Spirit and love that you shared with your books, poetry, but most importantly with your earth angel God driven Love.... I love you and miss you both immensely, Aunt Dorothy and Uncle Bruno.

And so I have a few words to share with you now about the most amazing and loving people I have ever known: Aunt Dorothy Holiday Thompson and Uncle Bruno Milinkovich, who have taught that our children are not our children, but God's children. And for your Translation efforts, Uncle Bruno, you made everything possible."Let Go And Let God": This book is made possible because you taught Isabella and Pat, Sara, and myself this invaluable lesson, to Let Go and Let God. This book is consistent because the both of you helped. And Lastly, Dorothy, with your relationship with the Queen, you helped in teaching us ethics that were not being taught in schools. You always said in dealing with a problem that something good will come out of it when you let go and let God. "How can it get better then this." Well, in great anticipation of all the wondrous things to become of this, I am thankful. With You All things are made Easy. I Love You. We are so glad our father and mother met you when they did in West Vancouver when we drove across Canada, Pat and Sara in their 20s and Isabella and I young and happy. We all shared such good times living in West Vancouver. You made things possible, and our father and mother learned immensely from you and passed it on with their love for each other. We know that was God's, let's say..."Little Gift." You have been a part of it ever since.

To ALL the relatives, you've been instrumental in sharing your love in the best way you know possible. Forgiveness is not always easy, yet Know you are always loved forever. We have grown together from our ability to stay closer to God within us all, and giving from that wealth within us. You are all such amazing Geniuses. Continue to do what you love, and know in doing so you are loved, supported, and Guided by God's infinite abundance. I Love you all tremendously and completely. You have all made your presence known with your Love.

And To my Godparents Luigi and Rosa Cassella ~ Your sense of humor and love for one another lives on in everyone's heart. You are loved and missed because you are both such humorous and fun people to be around. You care and understand in the best possible way you can, but most of all you genuinely love everybody for who they are, not what you think they should be. That makes a lot of people comfortable in your presence. Peter Loves you dearly forever! You make the greatest company. I can spend hours with you and still be laughing for days feeling your presence and love for one another, for your friends, my parents, and to all of your loved ones around you. Are you eating yet, to leave for Vancouver? I Love You!

To the Morenas: The love we share with one another and family feeling and friendship we share with all of the Morena family will continue to last over the infinite years to come. I miss you all so very much when I leave Montreal. Your hospitality and love is filled with only the kindest, unconditional Love I will ever know; one filled with honesty, integrity, commitment to loyalty and honor ~ You are all simply the best. And I know Isabella watches over you also for you made the Best Godparents she had ever had. Also, great cousins and friends you made us to become. Whoever knew, hey, Nick? Mary and Nick, your presence in Isabella's last days is never forgotten. It was actually so important. I am thankful, as we all are... And Joe, your love is sincere, honored, and respected by all. I Love you all so deeply ~ Robert and Vince, you're both so truly loved and admired for your spontaneity and missed dearly.

To Gerry Bruno: To a man who is a Mentor ~ Leader that I respect and admire for his commitment, dedication, and perseverance to Loving his family while pursuing his business purpose with an abundantly loving heart. Your invisible presence has been important in writing this book. You shared your way of life, habits, and business ethics, which

I have made my own. And I am eternally grateful for this, Gerry. You are an inspiration.

Divi Chanda, our conversations about love, care, and, most importantly, unconditional Love sparked further conversations that date Back on God, Spirit, and the Mind – You have indirectly helped as you know, Guided and helped in the process By doing what you Love. Yoga has Been Made into a Daily practice Because you chose to walk your talk – Ed and you have given inspiration just with your presence. You have made Yoga a part of so many people's lives. Thank you for being such dear friends....

Billy Thompson, you are missed yet. Our acting together and our friendship lasts forever. See you in your new Beverly Hills home, Mr. Hollywood ~ you're loved. I still have pancakes for you. What do you have? Our sense of humor will always stand tall with our friendship on the other side.

And to all the names who have been silently acknowledged in prayer and felt deeply in my Heart, "know you know" your presence has been felt in the process of this book and that you have all helped in this invaluable process. Know I am eternally and infinitely grateful in your guidance, in prayers, in your love and your speeches and silent conversation with God. I was always hearing your voices guiding me every step of the way. You know yourselves who have sent these silent conscious active and inactive moments with each other. You have all been in two places at the same time and have proven your presence in so many other ways. Your never-ending guidance and friendship is so dearly important.

Also, I feel it will take a lifetime and another book to acknowledge everyone who has contributed to this book's wealth – success.

To Elizabeth for encouraging and believing in the works that you haven't even seen ~ you are truly listening to God that resides in each one of us.

Bill and Beth Riedler, you wanted to See Me Succeed. You Both helped By Being yourselves And Doing what you know Best. I am eternally Grateful.

To Zio Giovanni and Zia Silvana Campologno for providing your home in Tuscany, Italy, to help create well-written books. Your home is the impetus of more tapes and books to come. And your Mickey Mouse picture in the room which I slept in made it possible to sleep like I was just back at home.... Zia and Zio, you have made your home feel like my own. Now how can it get better then this. You have been there for us all~ Isabella watches over you also.

Maria Gabriella, believe me, we are still having "Capellini" together in Italy and here all of the time ~ I love you and miss you in this world.

John Cain, Hilary Christine Woodward, Grace Normande Woodward: your invisible guidance and impeccable friendship mean more than you'll ever Know. All the long conversations, walks, and even time with Grace are so precious moments indeed. Our children are Gods children and you both exemplify and inspire everyone with your love for your daughter. Loving you all so Dearly.

Arlen Lorenzana, you made many of the Goals and God's plans possible with your home and refuge and loving support and friendship. You are all loved dearly.

To Mauzma, your friendship and guidance has been immensely important; in between editing and reading breaks you taught Peter to appreciate a glass of water, even before drinking it. God truly works through you with your love and inner strength.

Sabra Mott, your friendship and endless wisdom has helped in the process. God really brought us together in Victoria, and you made an important impact in all of our discussions and care to want to see me improve and be a great leader in business and especially in making this commitment to this very book.

* * * * *

To all those who were in the process of the Editing and Production and distribution of this book, you were eternally helpful. The storage, distribution, transportation and logistics, editing, and production of this book is just as important as the writing. We seem to think that writing a book is just that, writing a book, but it encompasses a lot more. Those who understand this process and have TRULY been there with their guidance, support, commitment, sincere generosity, and loyalty throughout the process have been True Friends indeed.

Gratitude and sincere appreciation is extended to Siva and Saikumar Varma and family for their contribution to the production of this book. To Katie, Susan Barr and Siva, "Your friendship and support have been important. You're Dearly Loved Forever. Also, since we met when we looked at each other from that window from the outside into the inside of the Ayurveda Center, "The Pacific Institute for Wholistic Living Inc" you and your whole family have shown what it means to love with care and compassion. You are all felt so fondly in Peter's heart and with smiles that we all radiate the room with constant love, light, and joy. Namaste." Our friendship Lasts Forever forever and ever with much respect and admirations.

Nigel Pike and Jacqui Pike for your help and attention to the technical editing of this book, "The Five Pillars of Relationships," and especially the blueprint for the added writing, the red for the editing of new words, and the rest of the technical suggestions you have given, Nigel. And Jacqui, for your impeccable strength and dedication with your intention to help in the process of this book and being a great neighborly friend. Your walks were healing, too, in maintaining clarity ~ God Bless You Both.

And Maureen Lauren for her help and lengthy hours of persistence to completion. You played a very important role in organizing the challenges to writing this book. You played the role of putting all the pieces of the book together, organizing everything beautifully. And your time, commitment, and loyalty in this process is so immensely appreciated, our conversations even more stimulating. You are dearly loved forever.

To Juliette Herdin as well for reading through and seeing what really needed to be changed with your never-ending support and efficiency. You are an amazing angel.

To Hugh Mcpherson for your neighborly support and friendship during some very difficult times.

Trevor, Akemi, Shon and Kent Oppelt your friendship means the world to Peter, and your love even more~ Domo Arigato Gozaimasu. It is fun to just talk and learn from walking in Friendship with each other. You were also wonderful neighbors at one time on Dallas Road, in Victoria; and then you gave so much of your love to Peter's parents during some great times together after you moved...even Kinoe~san enjoys your friendship.

Vicki Turner, Stenographer and Transcriber of one of the stages of the book: You elevated and read every word and page with Love. You are loved dearly. You are committed to loving others and building their self-esteem. You wish to see all prosper and have made this possible for so many. You are simply the best.... You've helped Me to Become a Better MAN.

And to all the Saints, Mothers, and Avatars in this world and Beautiful Angels that have Guided me along this Wonderful and Beautiful Process. "God's Guidance is Real. We Need only Seek it in our time Of Silence." "I LOVE YOU"

"I Love you Father as You Love ME"

Brenda Backer for her amazing Eye and Love for Photography and her healing work. What an amazing talent you have in Photography. I am enjoying your friendship and love immensely. Actually we are enjoying our friendship immensely. Your heart and talents amaze so many; Keep believing in yourself; you are one of the unsung heroes of the world, with you and your children. A Genius at Heart ~ I love you. You made this possible; and you gave hope and your full heart at the times when it was needed the most; your hands and Eyes are incredible talents; a Genius within you lives on and you give from that wealth; it is truly AMAZING! Our thoughts and feelings, are our prayers and you have mastered the art of the Eye and energy with incredible Genius!

Dave Fraser, you're a Genius with Computers. You can do wonders, and your friendship is cherished.

Barb Delph for your publicity efforts, time, and love for all. Keep Dreaming together and making a difference in peoples world with your publications~ thank you.

Jim Chapotelle, your friendship and Guidance is unspeakable and honored. With this computer you put together you made it possible to make these books, tapes, and videos all a vision and a fulfilled possibility. Your genius lives on among the sages as one of the greatest of all time. And to Dorie, Dylan, Devin, Aidan and family for allowing Jim the time. With your patience and love, you allowed him the freedom to help those he loves dearly. Your company, Linkatech.com is the success that you already are with your family and friends.

David Clarke, for your neighborly friendship bro, our talks, and being there for one another. It means the world... to be guided by your wisdom. Since we do not see each other often, I miss our conversations immensely.

Tammy Nelson, you are one of the greatest friends. You soothe Peter and have guided many aspects of this important Acknowledgement, Preface, Caveat, and Introduction to this book with your grammatical details and listening ear over many lengthy telephone calls in the middle of the morning and at night. You are truly cherished and loved.

Uncle Frank Sammarco, you made all the difference in people's lives. You were always laughing, never hurting anyone in your life! I miss you dearly in this life, Zio. You KNEW how to have fun and your smile and laughter always showed how you lived in the moment. You're still everyone's favorite uncle.

John Bede Harrison; you have been a dear friend for life and love you dearly always.

Michael O'Brien, you pushed me to do what I really love to do.

Dr. James McCreary and Dr. Smith, you have been there for our family at the most difficult times; you have always encouraged us all to do what we can, to be the best of who we really are. We Love you.

Pearl August for all of your talks in the process of writing this very book; we have laughed together and argued together and you have cheered me up "ole wise one".

Tony Parson, for mentioning and bringing up important issues on Beta Thalassemia Major on television. Thanks.

Peter's Grandparents, Maria Louisa and Vince Campolongo and Pietro and Maria Sammarco, you all have been so instrumental in Peter's upbringing. And To my great-grandparents and all the ancestors in this world who have helped and infinitely guided Peter to see through all the challenges that came about to make this all possible today. Your Infinite Guidance is so much appreciated at all times, with your unconditional love forever.

Uncle Mario Sammarco for your infinite friendship. You have been so instrumental in our conversations about The Five Pillars of Relationships.

Trafford Publishing for making this possible. And to all at Trafford Publishing who made this a reality with your assistance – your patience and persistence is remembered.

You have all been so friendly at the office that I wish we were all friends.

Dorothy and Sunset Services, without you this book would not be possible. You saw it through to the end. Your speed and commitment to quality is amazing. Your long friendship is even more important. You are loved dearly. You put together all of my great resumes, including the one that got me started into acting.

To Mystic Designs, Corey LeMay and Mark Anthony Sammarco, for creating such an amazing Web site and the time you have put in following your vision and doing what you love. Mark, your long hours and many creative details have made the book's cover Possible. We learned together. You are one amazing Godson ~ I love you. And to Corey LeMay for being a great leader.

Debbie Hara for continually creating your beautiful handmade cards. You have an incredible talent that heals the world. Your input to this book and your undivided attention and guidance have been invaluable to this book's wealth~success. Mahalo: You are a Genius who is loved.

Your one amazing creator of cards; and your friendship is cherished Forever. I love you. You have helped more then you imagined. Who would have thought all of this was possible but with your Genius within you that helps you and heals you as you heal the world with your amazing Genius. Keep creating those cards and making other's feel So GOOD!

Neil Goldhar, your presence has made a difference in everyone's lives. Thank you for sharing some of those moments in Vancouver, helping those who needed your friendship the most. We did A lot together.

Steven Goldhar and Sundance Media for your friendship and executive assistance. We laugh and smile together. You are a dear friend who is a Genius at what you do, yet still care to always seek the Truth. We are dear friends forever.

Ellen Beth Goldhar, your love and willingness to help this world is amazing – Your Praise is Generous and friendship even more important. I love you. If there is one person who can make this world shine, it is you. You make everyone feel good and put smiles on people's faces with your infinite love.

To a Dear Man, Wayne W. Dyer, a few years ago you sent Peter Two books, "What Do you Really Want For your children?", and you wrote, "Peter Teach Only Love" This has resonated for years. You guided Peter and gave Love, Life and Laughter when all others were judging instead of Loving – You GAVE life where others ignored life as only Being circumstance - instead you challenged everyone to See Love in all that we do, see, touch and SPEAK. You are the Father of Inspiration. And you have Given life not taken life – You have done what matters most and you have aspired to achieve the following: "People Don't Care How Much I know until they know How Much I CARE" And, "Promise a lot, But Deliver Even More" You are doing more then you are willing to Acknowledge; you have reached a great Seeing Satori. Peter dearly Loves you, as do his parents. You are dearly loved Wayne, and your contribution to this book is felt with your "Spiritual Presence." You Give and you give and you give your love~ I feel your presence many times...Loving you always, Namaste.

Louise Hay, you have made it possible for Peter's Dreams to come true; with your seminars in Las Vegas, he has been able to share his love, and his book with others. The Hay house family is truly one who cares. Louise you've given hope to so many and your books have been used widely in creating happy lives to Millions. I love you & you Are Something Special. We need to keep healing each others lives. You are truly a Genius of Love.

Dearest Kaye and Edwarda O'Bara your unconditional love and your loving spiritual presence is felt amongst the miles. You truly have shown what it means to love other people; I love you Dearly!

Joe Ruthkowski, for your inspiring words and reasoning phone calls made much of this writing possible just for caring.

Keith and Linda Faye: your encouragement and love lives on in these pages of this book.

Jenny, even all the way from Australia, you still inspire with your love and spirit ~ I love you.

To Leon and Elizabeth Pearson: For buying one of the very first book releases!

Azim Jamal: your friendship and mentoring means the world to me; I enjoy your love and light immensely.

Dearest Deepak Chopra, you have given So Many chances to So Many others, But Back on November 10th, 1999, Peter Wrote a poem in his office one evening, called WE ARE ONE, in a matter of minutes; and then, the next day Peter sent this poem to you as well as your dear friend Wayne - in return you and your administration staff at The Chopra Center sent Peter a post card letter, stating, that you wanted to put the poem We Are One into your community website. I was flattered, and in awe of it all~! It was the beginning of a continued intention to write as many books as possible until you hold this very "one" in your hands. This is what you truly call, "Infinite Patience's Producing immediate Results" You are seeding the helper who made it possible to continue this path of creating infinite patience with the Infinite Source and Supply we call Love, and in the service of making others happy. This Comes in Just coming from one persons vision. Thank you for Caring for Peter's Vision, while you continue to maintain your Dreams. Namaste.

Michael J Fox, Thank you for BEING there for my Sister Isabella Maria Sammarco in the summer of 1986, before she died on July 29th; you gave her the love and willingness to let go and live again.

Johnny Depp: You Truly were there for me when starting my acting career and gave me hope and great contacts in the process as well. You have been thought of ever since in your guidance, indispensable advice and direction. You knew how to be a Friend to others by being one Yourself.

I wish to say thank you to so many other people and I apologize if I have missed any names along the way. This has not been my intent.

Dr. Szuson Wong thank you for giving Peter a chance to be in your In Touch magazine. This has helped immensely, more then you will ever know; your silence and invisible help will continue to come very much back to you too. You are appreciated for all of your efforts. With Much Love....

Marianne Williamson, you are loved dearly and felt in my heart always. Much love to everyone at the office.

Talking about you Brother Peter at The Power Within in Vancouver while back stage during Sylvia Browne. Talk was the beginning of a wonderful connect between each other – thank you.

And finally, to Humanity, which is our family. You have all contributed to making this book possible.

ABOUT THE AUTHOR:

Who is Peter?

To Know **Peter Sammarco** is to know a man whose intention is to touch in a positive way as many lives as he can. To help those he meets understand who they are, to help empower them to reach their fullest potential.

He wishes to seed only the good, and we need to see only the good in others. Despite Isabella's death, the family learned how to live in the moment, love in the moment, and forgive in this very moment.

Peter's Sense of humor and Style with words and care and Love to all shows in his actions and in his presence.

Contact us for any products, services, or 'relationship building':

www. FivePillars.ca
www.HealYourSelf.ca
Telephone 250-382-9397

Be The Creator of Your Own World.

In this remarkable book lies the secrets to creating inner peace. Here you will discover the joy of loving others by first loving who you really are within. Knowing your heart is the revealer of who you are and the shielder of anger, resentment and harbored hate.

In fact Peter Sammarco explores the full meaning of loving, trusting, knowing, mastering and Giving Thyself through the power of – Forgiving Thyself and creating the fulfillment of abundance of peace and joy in your life by understanding these great secret pillars ~with Love.

Knowing you can create anything in your world *The Five Pillars of Relationships* fosters the steps and guidance to fulfilling anything in your own world, with simple steps and actions that can be understood by all. ~"It is in loving ourselves that we are truly rich."

"When we love, we grow—

Love Thyself. Give Thyself—"When we give, it teaches you have more to give".

Master Thyself— "OUR attitudes CAN heal anything when we make a shift in our "thinking" we can make even further shifts in our feelings. What we know to be true in our hearts is what we feel in our bodies…"

© Copyright 2004-2005, Peter Sammarco.

ISBN 1-41205291-2